Conten

Welcome to
Step 1

S s

ACTION

Weave your hand in an ‹s› shape like a snake, and say *sssss*.

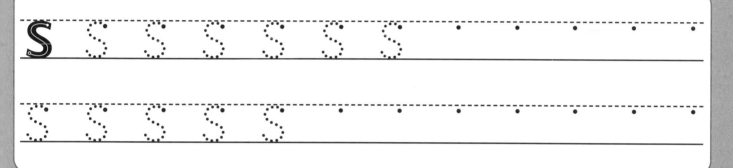

S

Say the word for each picture. Three have a /s/ sound at the beginning. Cross out the one that does not.

3

A a

ACTION

Wiggle your fingers up your arm as if ants are crawling on you, and say *a, a, a, a!*

a a a a a a · · · · ·

a s a s a s · · · · ·

S

a

Say the word for each picture. Three have an /a/ sound at the beginning. Cross out the one that does not.

T t

ACTION

Turn your head from side to side as if you are watching tennis, and say *t, t, t, t.*

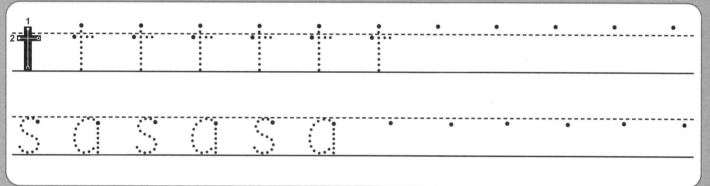

at

sat

Say the word for each picture. Three have a /t/ sound at the beginning. Cross out the one that does not.

I i

ACTION

Wiggle your fingers at the end of your nose as if you are a mouse stroking its whiskers, and squeak *i, i, i, i*.

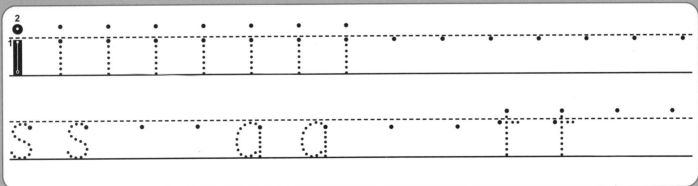

it

sit

Say the word for each picture. Three have an /i/ sound at the beginning. Cross out the one that does not.

P p

ACTION

Hold up your finger as if it is a candle and pretend to puff it out, saying p, p, p, p.

p p p p p

ss a a t t i i

pit

pat

tip

tap

Say the word for each picture. Three have a /p/ sound at the beginning. Cross out the one that does not.

N n

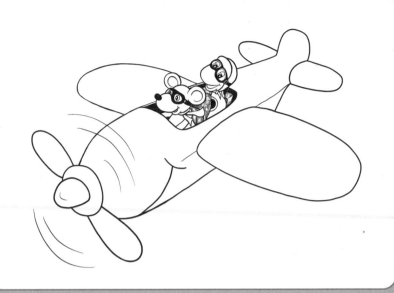

ACTION

Pretend to be a plane with your arms out like wings, and say *nnnnnn*.

n n n n n n n

a   t   i   p

tin

ant

nip

pan

Say the word for each picture. Three have a /n/ sound at the beginning. Cross out the one that does not.

Cc Kk

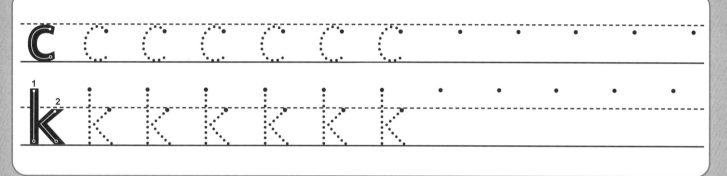

c

k

kit

cap

pick

sack

Say the word for each picture and write the letter for the first sound. Three start with caterpillar /c/ or kicking /k/, but one does not.

c

c

k

p

E e

ACTION

Pretend to crack an egg against the side of a pan with one hand. Use both hands to open the shell, saying e, e, e, e.

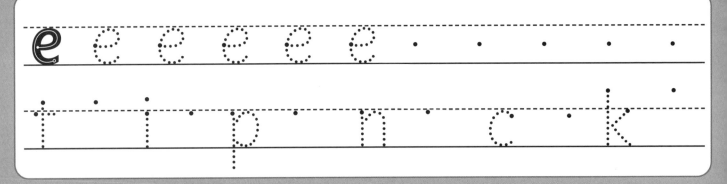

ten

pet

tent

neck

Say the word for each picture and write the letter for the first sound. Three start with /e/, but one does not.

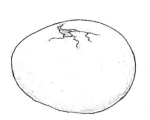

_____

_____

_____

_____

H h

ACTION

Hold your hand up to your mouth as if you are out of breath, and say *h, h, h, h.*

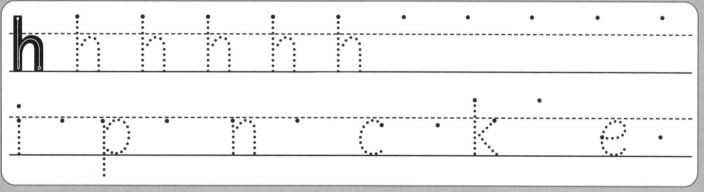

hip

hat

hen

hiss

Say the word for each picture and write the letter for the first sound. Three start with /h/, but one does not.

11

R r

ACTION

Pretend to be a puppy pulling a rag and shake your head from side to side, saying *rrrrrr*.

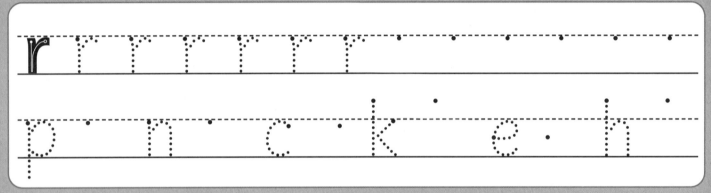

rip

rat

rest

trap

Say the word for each picture and write the letter for the first sound. Three start with /r/, but one does not.

M m

ACTION

Rub your tummy as if you can see some tasty food, and say *mmmmmm*.

m m m m m

r c k e h r

men

him

miss

man

Say the word for each picture and write the letter for the first sound. Three start with /m/, but one does not.

D d

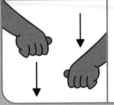

ACTION

Move your hands up and down as if you are beating a drum, and say d, d, d, d.

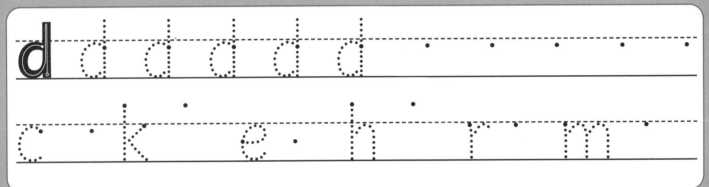

dip

red

dad

hand

Say the word for each picture and write the letter for the first sound. Three start with /d/, but one does not.

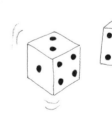

G g

ACTION

Move your hand in a downward spiral like water gurgling down a drain, and say *g, g, g, g.*

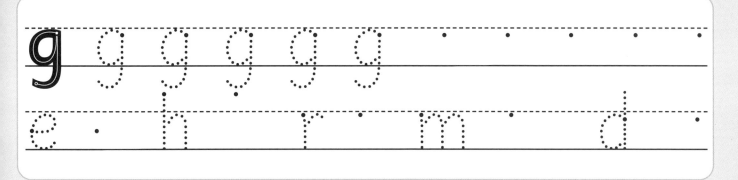

egg

dig

peg

grin

Say the word for each picture. Three have a /g/ sound in them. Cross out the one that does not.

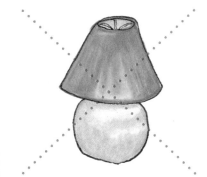

O o

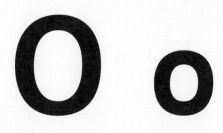

ACTION

Pretend to turn a light switch on and off, and say *o-o, o-o*.

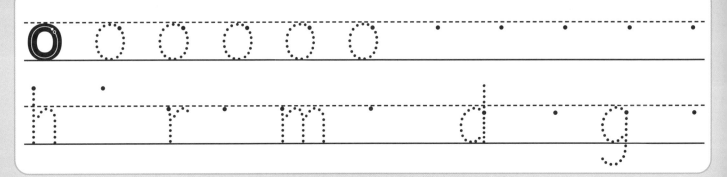

hot

dog

hop

socks

Say the word for each picture. Three have an /o/ sound in them. Cross out the one that does not.

U u

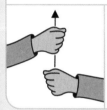

ACTION

Keep one hand steady and raise the other as if putting up an umbrella, and say *u, u, u, u.*

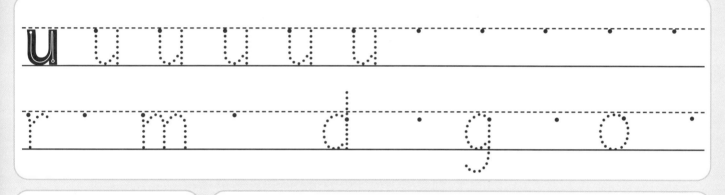

u u u u u u

r m d g o

up

sun

mud

truck

Say the word for each picture. Three have an /u/ sound in them. Cross out the one that does not.

17

L l

ACTION

Pretend to lick a lollipop, saying *lllll*.

l l l l l l l l l l l l l l l l l l l

m d g o u

leg

lips

doll

help

Say the word for each picture. Three have a /l/ sound in them. Cross out the one that does not.

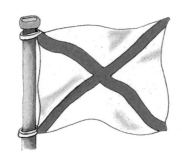

F f

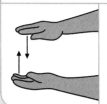

ACTION

Slowly bring your hands together to mime an inflatable fish deflating, and say *fffff*.

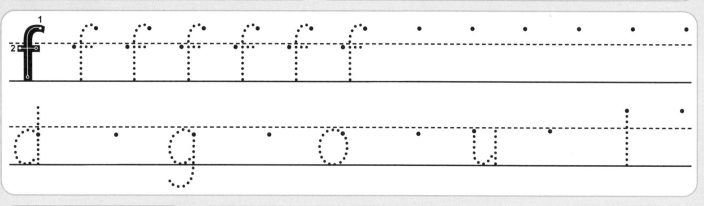

fit

· · ·

fun

· · ·

puff

· · ·

soft

· · · ·

Say the word for each picture. Three have a /f/ sound in them. Cross out the one that does not.

B b

ACTION

Pretend to hit a ball with a bat, saying *b, b, b, b.*

b b b b b b

d g o u t f

big

bag

bell

crab

Say the word for each picture. Three have a /b/ sound in them. Cross out the one that does not.

ai

ACTION

Cup your hand over your ear as if you are trying to hear something, and say *ai*?

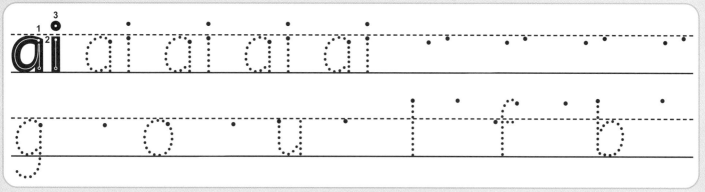

rain

tail

snail

paint

Look at each picture and say the sounds in the word. Write the letters for the /ai/ sound in the correct dot.

J j

ACTION

Pretend to wobble like jello on a plate, saying *j, j, j, j.*

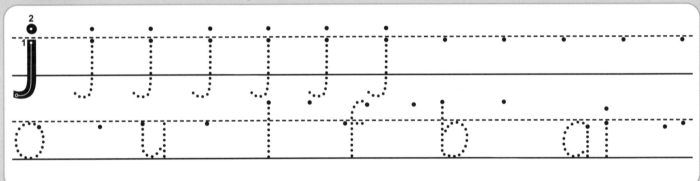

jet

jog

just

jump

Look at each picture and say the sounds in the word. Write the letter for the /j/ sound in the correct dot.

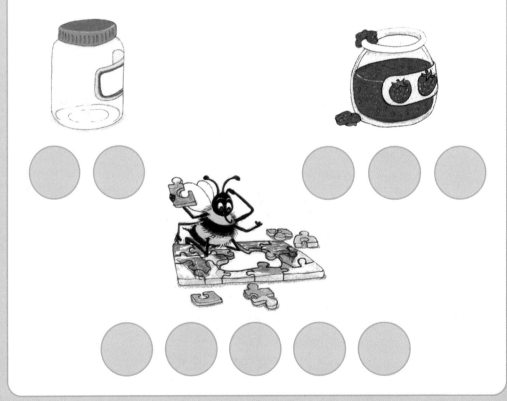

oa

ACTION

Bring your hand over your mouth as if something has gone wrong, and say *oa!*

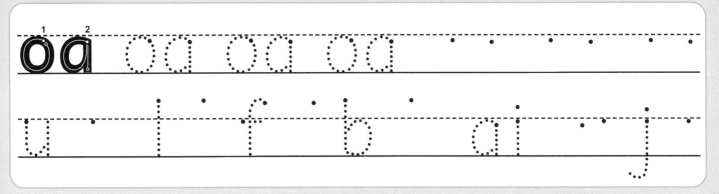

goat

road

soap

toast

Look at each picture and say the sounds in the word. Write the letters for the /oa/ sound in the correct dot.

ie

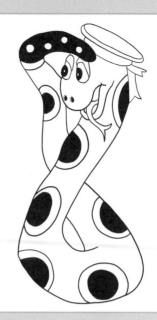

ACTION

Salute as if you are a sailor, saying *ie-ie*.

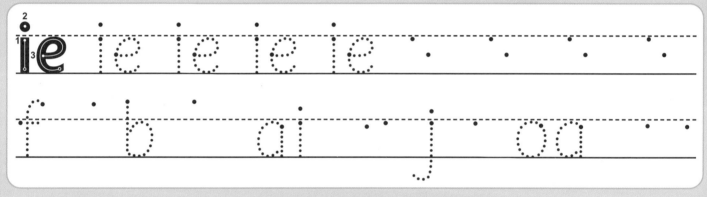

ie ie ie ie ie

f b ai j oa

lie

tied

untie

magpie

Look at each picture and say the sounds in the word. Write the letters for the /ie/ sound in the correct dot.

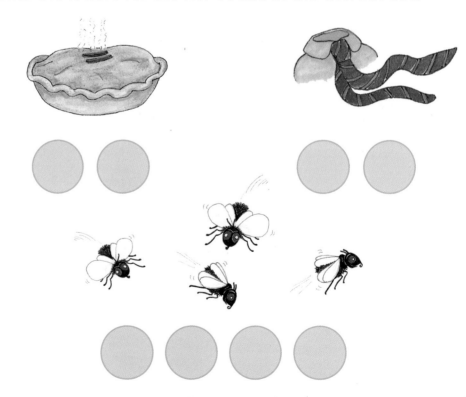

ee or

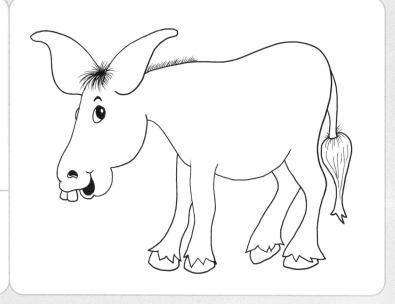

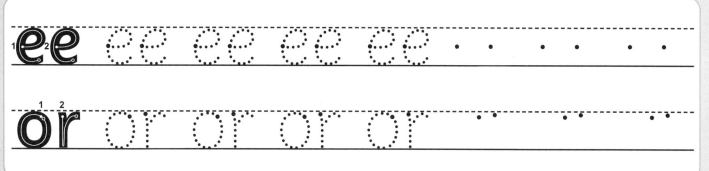

ee ee ee ee ee . . . .

or or or or or . . . . . .

bee
tree
sleep

corn
fork
storm

Look at each picture and say the sounds in the word. Write the letters for the /ee/ or /or/ sound in the correct dot.

Z z

ACTION

Put your arms out at your sides and flap them like a bee, saying zzzzzz.

z zzzzzzzz

oa ie ee or

zap
· · ·

buzz
· · ·

fizz
· · ·

unzip
· · · · ·

Say the sounds in the word for each picture and color in the correct number of dots. Cross out the one that does not have a /z/ sound in it.

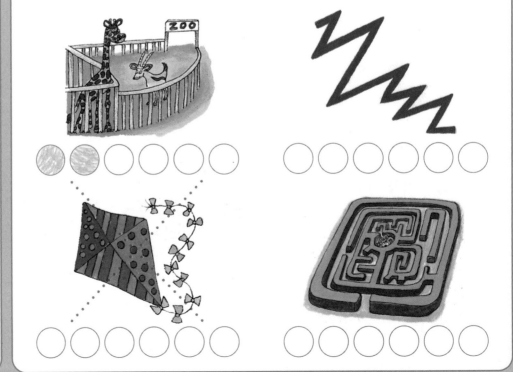

W w

ACTION

Blow onto your open hands as if you are the wind, saying *w, w, w, w*.

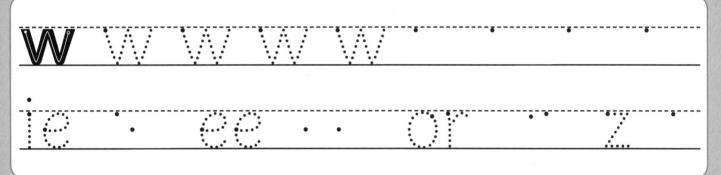

w w w w

ie ee or z

web
• • •

twig
• • • •

week
• • • •

wind
• • • •

Say the sounds in the word for each picture and color in the correct number of dots. Cross out the one that does not have a /w/ sound in it.

27

ng

ACTION

Pretend to be a weightlifter lifting a heavy weight above your head, and say *ng...*

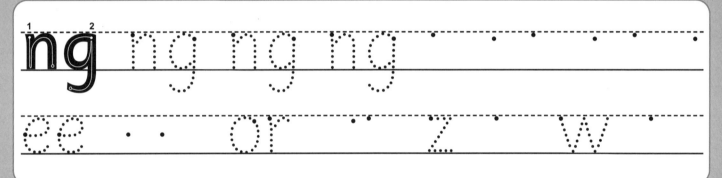

ng ng ng ng

ee · · or ·· z w

sing
· · · ·

long
· · · ·

bang
· · · ·

strong
· · · · ·

Say the sounds in the word for each picture and color in the correct number of dots. Cross out the one that does not have a /ng/ sound in it.

V v

ACTION

Pretend to be driving along in a van, saying *vvvvvv*.

v v v v v v v v

or   z   w   ng

vet
· · ·

van
· · ·

vest
· · · ·

seven
· · · · ·

Say the sounds in the word for each picture and color in the correct number of dots. Cross out the one that does not have a /v/ sound in it.

◯◯◯◯◯

◯◯◯◯◯

◯◯◯◯◯

◯◯◯◯◯

29

oo OO

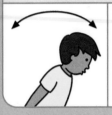

ACTION

Move your head back and forth like the cuckoo in a cuckoo clock, calling *oo-oo, oo-oo* (*oo* as in book, *oo* as in moon).

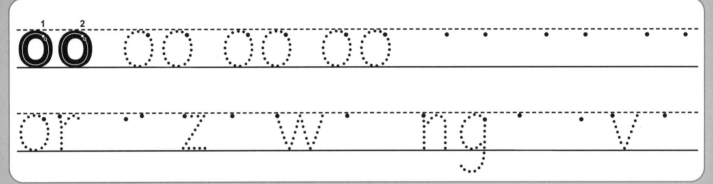

oo oo oo oo

or   z   w   ng   v

foot
look
good

zoo
pool
moon

Say the sounds in the word for each picture and color in the correct number of dots. Cross out the ones that do not have an /oo/ or /oo/ sound in them.

◯◯◯◯   ◯◯◯◯   ◯◯◯◯

◯◯◯◯   ◯◯◯◯   ◯◯◯◯

Y y

ACTION

Pretend to eat yogurt from a spoon, saying y, y, y, y.

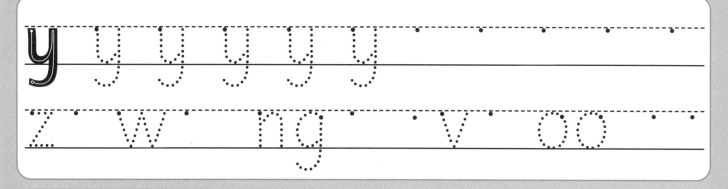

yes

yak

yell

yelp

Color in the correct number of sounds for each word. Write the letter for the /y/ sound in the correct dot.

X x

ACTION

Pretend to take an x-ray with an x-ray camera, saying *ks, ks, ks, ks*.

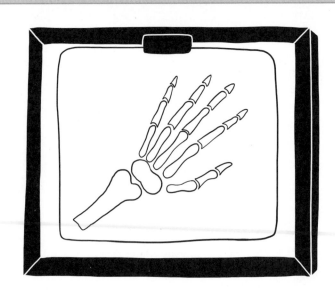

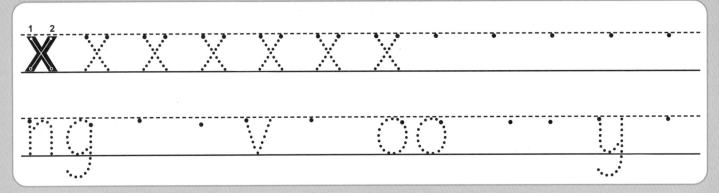

box
· · ·

mix
· · ·

exit
· · · ·

next
· · · ·

Color in the correct number of sounds for each word. Write the letter for the /x/ sound in the correct dot.

ch

ACTION

Move your arms at your sides like a steam train, saying *ch, ch, ch, ch*.

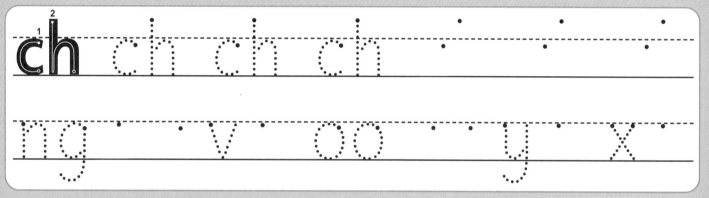

ch ch ch ch

ng   v   oo   y   x

chop

chain

torch

bunch

Color in the correct number of sounds for each word. Write the letters for the /ch/ sound in the correct dot.

sh

ACTION

Place your index finger against your lips, and say *shshshsh*.

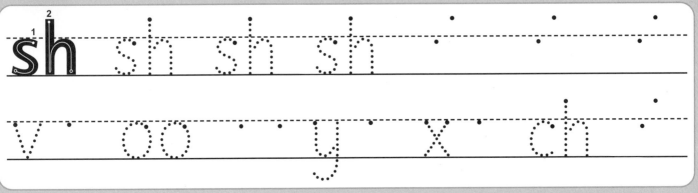

sh sh sh sh

v oo y x ch

dish

shop

sheep

brush

Color in the correct number of sounds for each word. Write the letters for the /sh/ sound in the correct dot.

th th

ACTION

Pretend to be a rude clown. Stick out your tongue a little for *th* (as in *this*) and further for *th* (as in *thumb*).

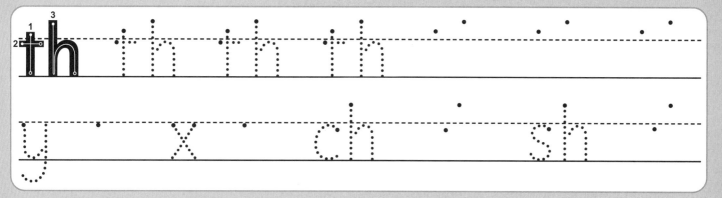

th   th   th   th

y   x   ch   sh

this

that

then

thin

moth

three

Color in the correct number of sounds for each word. Write the letters for the /th/ or /th/ sound in the correct dot.

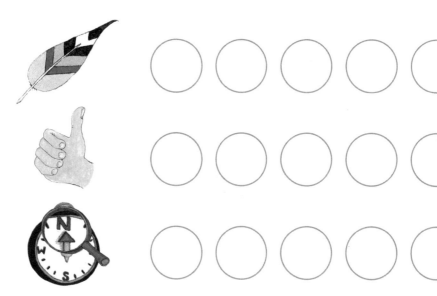

◯ ◯ ◯ ◯ ◯

◯ ◯ ◯ ◯ ◯

◯ ◯ ◯ ◯ ◯

◯ ◯ ◯ ◯ ◯

Qu qu

ACTION

Make a duck's beak with your hands and open and close it, saying *qu, qu, qu, qu.*

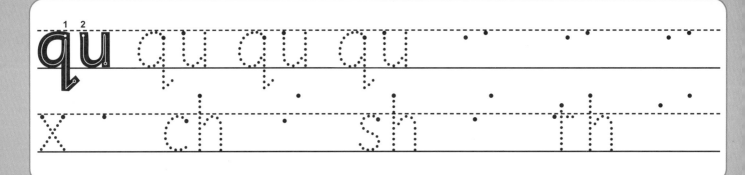

qu qu qu qu

x   ch   sh   th

quiz

· · · ·

squid

· · · ·

quack

·   ·

squirrel

· · · ·

Look at each picture and say the sounds in the word. Write the letters for the /qu/ sound in the correct dot.

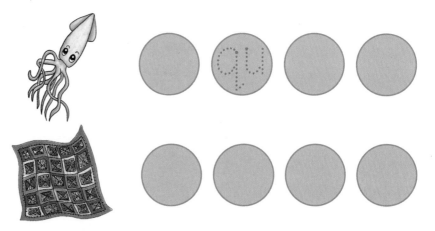

Write the word for the picture. Remember to listen for all the sounds in the word.

qu ee n

36

ou

ACTION

Pretend your finger is a needle and prick your thumb, saying *ou!*

ou ou ou ou

ch · sh · th · qu

out
loud
shout
mouth

Look at each picture and say the sounds in the word. Write the letters for the /ou/ sound in the correct dot.

Write the word for the picture. Remember to listen for all the sounds in the word.

____ ____ ____ ____

oi

ACTION

Cup your hands around your mouth as if you are hailing a passing boat, and say *oi, ship ahoy!*

oi oi oi oi oi

sh th qu ou

oil

join

soil

point

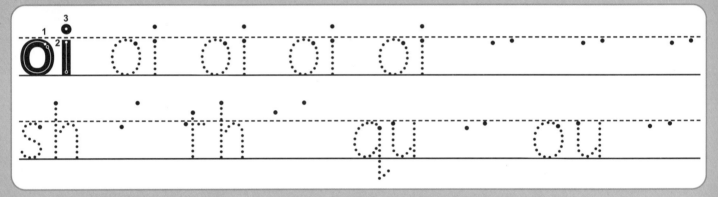

Look at each picture and say the sounds in the word. Write the letters for the /oi/ sound in the correct dot.

Write the word for the picture. Remember to listen for all the sounds in the word.

___ ___ ___

38

ue

ACTION

Point to people around you, and say *ue, ue, ue, ue*.

ue ue ue ue

th qu ou oi

fuel
· · ·

value
· · · ·

statue
· · · · ·

continue
· · · · · · ·

Look at each picture and say the sounds in the word. Write the letters for the /ue/ sound in the correct dot.

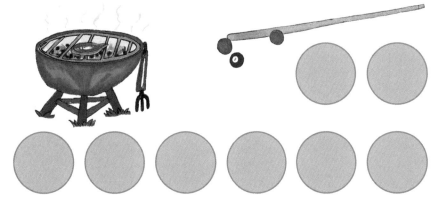

○ ○

○ ○ ○ ○ ○ ○

Write the word for the picture. Remember to listen for all the sounds in the word.

_ _ _ _ _ _

39

er

to
do

ACTION

Roll your hands over each other like a mixer, and say *er-er-er-er*.

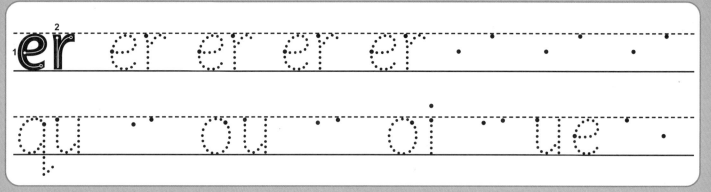

er er er er er · · · · ·

qu · ou · oi · ue ·

letter
· · · ·

number
· · · ·

winter
· · · ·

summer
· · · ·

Look at each picture and say the sounds in the word. Write the letters for the /er/ sound in the correct dot.

Write the word for the picture. Remember to listen for all the sounds in the word.

_____ _____ _____ _____

ar

are
all

ACTION

Clap your hands loosely like a seal, and say *ar, ar, ar, ar.*

ar ar ar ar ar

ou oi ue er

jar

dark

shark

farmer

Look at each picture and say the sounds in the word. Write the letters for the /ar/ sound in the correct dot.

Write the word for the picture. Remember to listen for all the sounds in the word.

41

Tricky Words 1

Read the words and underline the tricky bit.

Now try writing them. Say the word each time, listen for the sounds, and remember how to write the tricky bit.

Look Find the tricky bit.	Copy then Cover	Write then Check	Have another go!
the	the		
he	he		
she	she		
me	me		
we	we		
be	be		

Tricky Words 2

Read the words and underline the tricky bit.

Now try writing them. Say the word each time, listen for the sounds, and remember how to write the tricky bit.

Look Find the tricky bit.	Copy then Cover	Write then Check	Have another go!
I	I		
was	was		
to	to		
do	do		
are	are		
all	all		

Reading and Writing

1 Read the words and draw a picture for each one.

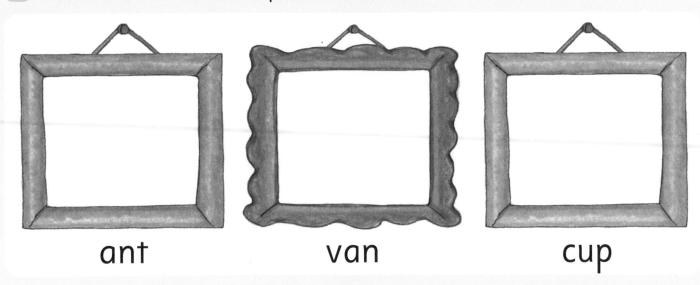

ant   van   cup

2 Choose the right word and write it underneath the picture. Color the pictures in.

met mat man
m a t

log dig dog
_ _ _

sun run fun
_ _ _

pet hen pen
_ _ _

net nut not
_ _ _

fix six fox
_ _ _

three trick tree
_ _ _ _ _

boot book boat
_ _ _ _

shark arm farm
_ _ _ _ _

3 Read each word and match it to the right picture. Color the pictures in.

fork   dog   bus

mixer   statue

coin   bed   yak

4 Read these tricky words. Can you find them hidden below?

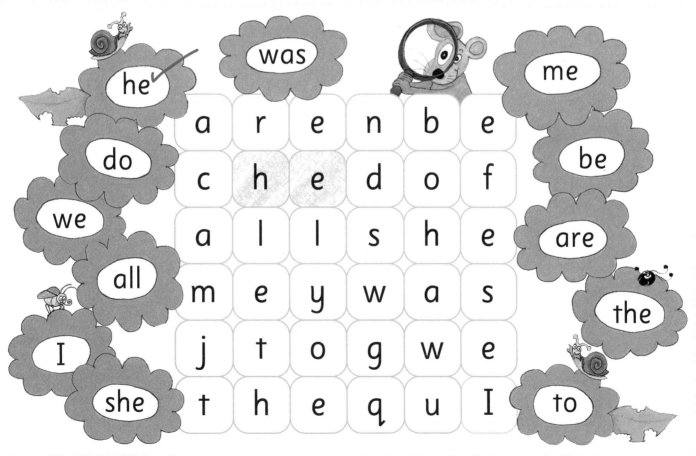

he   was   me

do   be

we   are

all

a	r	e	n	b	e
c	h	e	d	o	f
a	l	l	s	h	e
m	e	y	w	a	s
j	t	o	g	w	e
t	h	e	q	u	I

I

she   the   to

5 Read the sentences and draw a picture for each one.

This is me.

I can run.

6 Look at the pictures and write the words underneath.

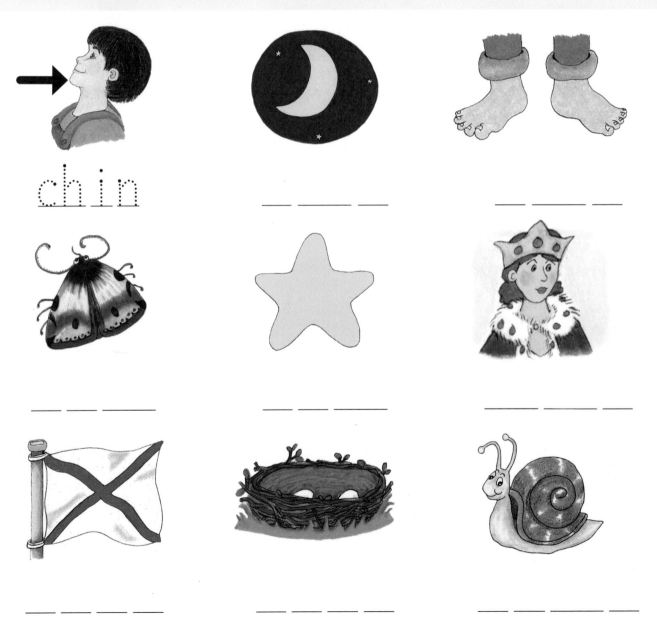

ch i n

___ ___ ___

___ ___ ___

___ ___ ___

___ ___ ___

___ ___ ___

___ ___ ___ ___

___ ___ ___

___ ___ ___ ___ ___

7 Read the sentences and draw a picture for each one.

He can sing.

She was sad.

I can jump.

We all hop.

The sun is hot.

Drums are loud.

8 Fill in the missing words to complete these sentences.

The _____ is hot.

 The _____ croaks.

The _____ is big.

 The _____ buzzes.

9 Fill in the missing words and color each picture to match the sentence.

 The _____ is black.

I see the green _____.

 We need pink _____.

The _____ is red.

Well done!

Now you know these letter sounds and tricky words.

s a t i c k e h r
p n m d
g ai j
o u oa
f b ie
z w are was ee or
y x
ng all ch
v oo sh th
qu ou oi ue er ar

49

Welcome to Step 2

y as /ee/

In these words the ‹y› at the end makes an /ee/ sound.

silly   happy   muddy   jelly

party   funny   daddy   spotty

Read the words in the logs. Match each word to the right picture.

sunny

body

puppy

teddy

sandy

holly

Handwriting

s · · ·

a · · ·

t · ·

i · · ·

p · · ·

n · · ·

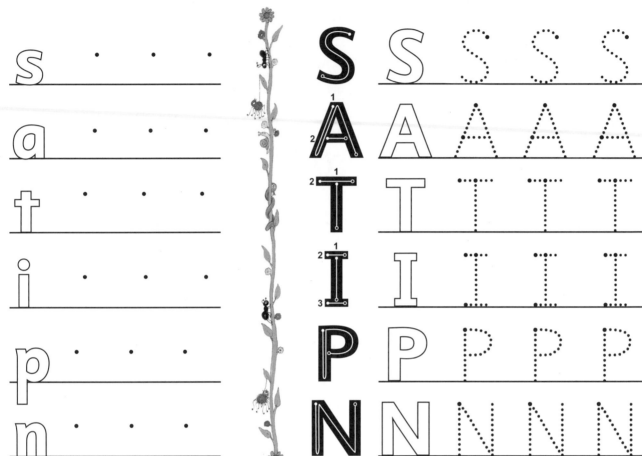

S S S S S S

A A A A A A A

T T T T T T T

I I I I I I I

P P P P P P P

N N N N N N N

Write inside the outline letters and match each capital letter to its lower-case letter.

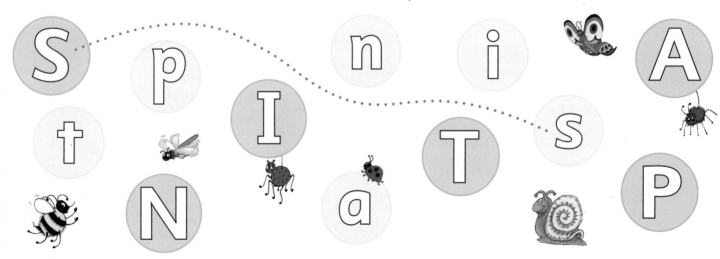

S p n i A
t I s
N a T P

Write the capital letter for each of these lower-case letters.

a A   p ___   i ___   s ___   n ___   t ___

Look Find the tricky bit.	Copy then Cover	Write then Check	Have another go!
you	you		
your	your		

Words and Sentences

the hen

_____

_____

_____

_____

53

Short Vowels

 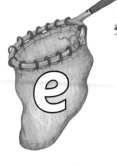   

a   e   i   o   u

bag   net   bin   box   mug

Identify the short vowel and write the word. Color the pictures.

a e i **o** u

b o x

a e i o u

_ _ _

a e i o u

_ _ _ _

a e i o u

_ _ _ _

a e i o u
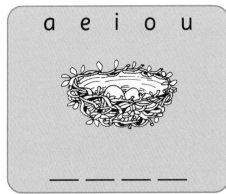
_ _ _ _

a e i o u

_ _ _ _

a e i o u

_ _ _

a e i o u

_ _ _

a e i o u
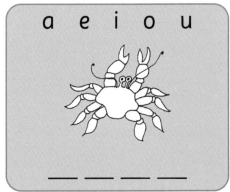
_ _ _ _

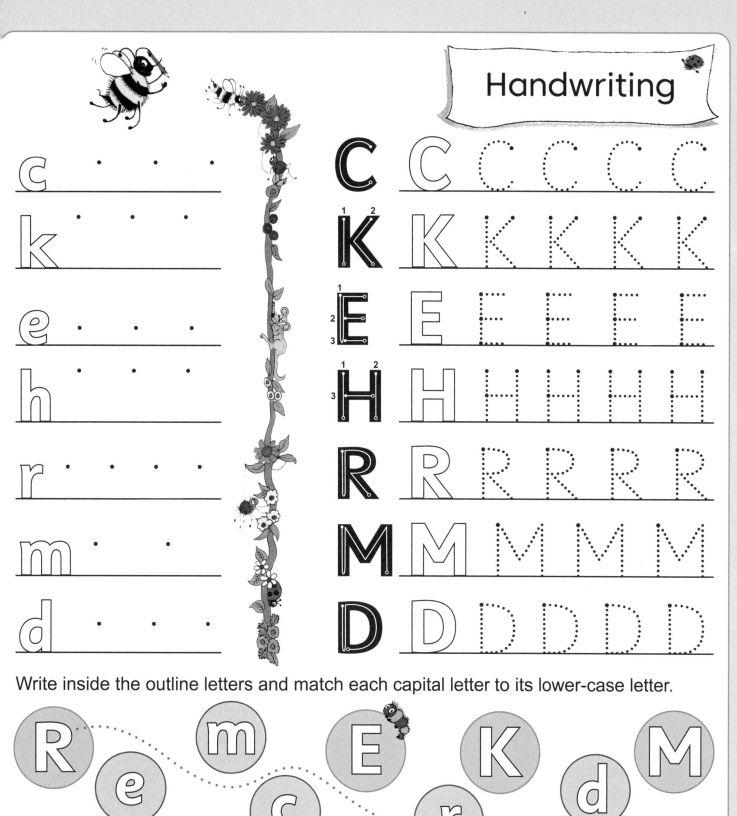

c _____

k _____

e _____

h _____

r _____

m _____

d _____

C C C C C C

K K K K K K

E E E E E E

H H H H H H

R R R R R R

M M M M M M

D D D D D D

Write inside the outline letters and match each capital letter to its lower-case letter.

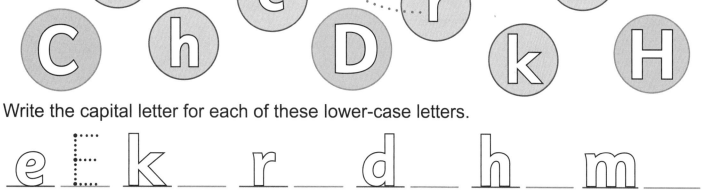

R e m E K M
C h c D r d k H

Write the capital letter for each of these lower-case letters.

e E   k ____   r ____   d ____   h ____   m ____

come

Tricky Words

some

Look Find the tricky bit.	Copy then Cover	Write then Check	Have another go!
come	come		
some	some		

Words and Sentences

in the park

ck

Caterpillar /c/ and kicking /k/ are both needed in words with a short vowel sound.

luck   check   sack   peck   truck

rock   jacket   tick   kick   clock

Write over the dotted words and draw a picture for each word in the rockets.

g
o
u
l
f
b

G G G G G G
O O O O O O
U U U U U U
L L L L L L
F F F F F F
B B B B B B

Write inside the outline letters and match each capital letter to its lower-case letter.

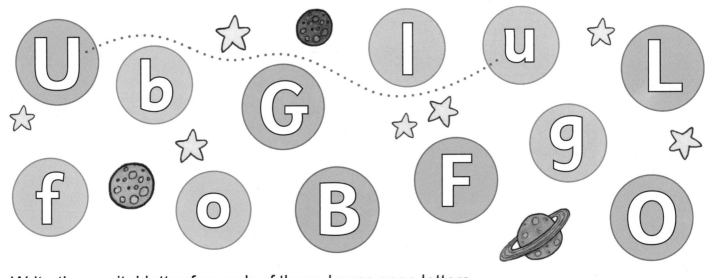

Write the capital letter for each of these lower-case letters.

u U   g   l   o   b   f

Tricky Words

said here there

Look Find the tricky bit.	Copy then Cover	Write then Check	Have another go!
said	said		
here	here		
there	there		

Words and Sentences

on the pond

_____

_____

_____

Double Letters

When two letters that make the same sound are next to each other, the sound is only said once.

| parrot | egg | bell | add | button |

| kitten | buzz | toffee | doll | miss |

Read the words in the rabbit and draw a picture for each one.

rabbit

dinner

dress

shell

puppet

carrot

Write the lower-case ‹j› and its capital ‹J›. Then write inside the vowel digraphs.

j   •   •   •   •   _____   J J J J J J J J J

ai   oa   ie   ee   or

Write inside each capital letter and join it to its matching lower-case letter.

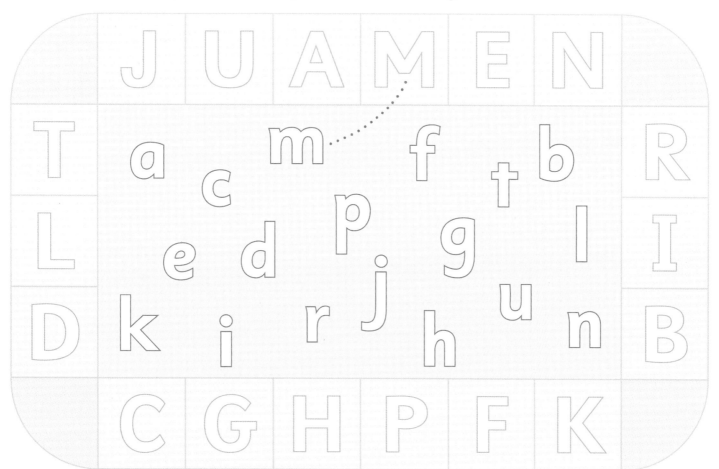

Write the capital letter for each of these lower-case letters.

S   a   c   o   f   j

Tricky Words

they

Look Find the tricky bit.	Copy then Cover	Write then Check	Have another go!
they	they		

Words and Sentences

the fox

_____

_____

_____

Magic e

The final ‹e› in the spellings below does not say its sound. Instead, it uses its magic to hop back over the consonant and turns the short vowel into a long vowel sound.

a_e   e_e   i_e   o_e   u_e

Add a magic ‹e› to complete each word. Then color the pictures.

bike   rose   mule

gate   Eve   five

mole   cake   cube

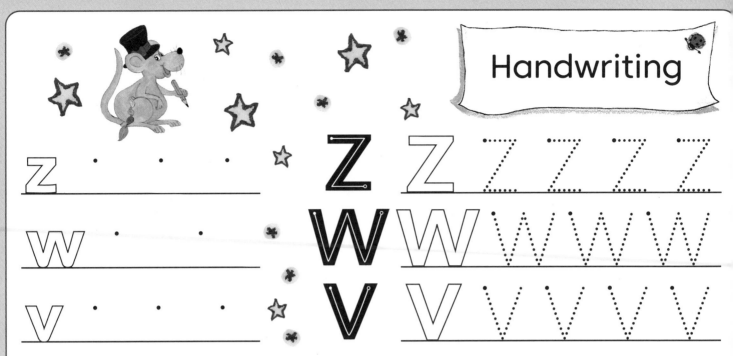

Handwriting

z _____

w _____

v _____

Z Z Z Z Z Z Z Z

W W W W W W W

V V V V V V V V

Write inside each outline letter and then write its matching capital or lower-case letter next to it.

s S ___

A ___

i ___

T ___

P ___

n ___

K ___

c ___

e ___

h ___

R ___

m ___

d ___

Tricky Words

go   no   so

Look Find the tricky bit.	Copy then Cover	Write then Check	Have another go!
go	go		
no	no		
so	so		

Words and Sentences

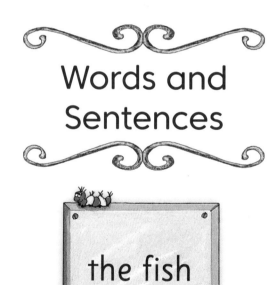

the fish

_____

_____

_____

_____

Long Vowels

The long vowel sounds /ai/, /ee/, /ie/, /oa/, and /ue/ can also be written ‹a_e›, ‹e_e›, ‹i_e›, ‹o_e›, and ‹u_e›. These spellings have a magic ‹e› and are called hop-over ‹e› digraphs.

smoke   use   game   eve   mule

hive   these   joke   shave   side

Join each leaf to the right tree.

Pete   bone   smile   plane   cube   nose   skate   rope   kite

Handwriting

Write inside each outline letter and then write its matching capital or lower-case letter next to it.

 my

 Tricky Words

 one

 by

Look Find the tricky bit.	Copy then Cover	Write then Check	Have another go!
my	my		
one	one		
by	by		

 Words and Sentences

 in the dark

_____

_____

_____

Alternatives

Write inside the vowel letters using a blue pen or pencil. Then look at the grid and color the squares with a short vowel in blue.

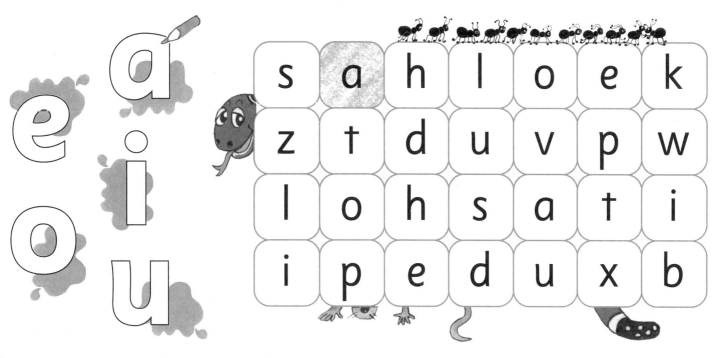

Choose the right word and write it underneath the picture.

cub   cube

fin   fine

hop   hope

_____

_____

_____

pet   Pete

hat   hate

plan   plane

_____

_____

_____

69

Words and Sentences

Step 2 Units 1 and 2   Join each word to the right picture.

chick   hen   nest   egg

dog   tree   swing   picnic

Step 2 Units 3 and 4   Join each word to the right picture.

toad   boat   duckling   rocks

red   tail   fox   bat

Words and Sentences / Tricky Words

Step 2 Units 5 and 6 Join each word to the right picture.

starfish   flatfish   eel   catfish

star   moon   moth   sleeping

Step 2 Unit 4 Read the tricky words. Can you find them hidden below?

you								here
your								some
said								they
there								come

a	c	o	m	e	b	o	s
s	a	i	d	d	t	p	f
o	q	p	a	y	o	u	m
h	e	r	e	c	d	x	z
q	u	m	t	h	e	r	e
y	o	u	r	f	h	o	u
k	s	j	x	t	h	e	y
c	z	s	o	m	e	r	w

Handwriting

Step 2   Units 1 to 6   Say the alphabet. Point to each letter as you say it.

Aa Bb Cc Dd Ee

Ff Gg Hh Ii Jj
Kk Ll Mm

Nn Oo Pp Qq Rr Ss

Tt Uu Vv Ww
Xx Yy Zz

Well done!
Now you know the alphabet